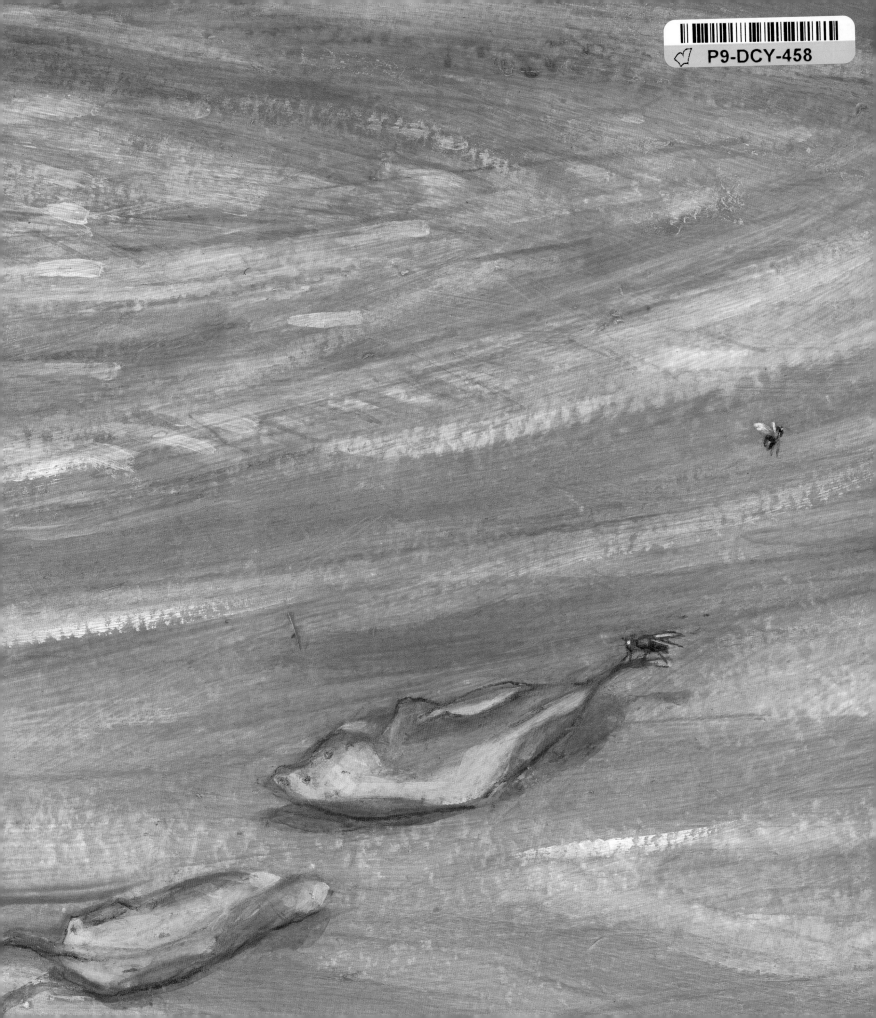

For Jenny
S. W.

To Ninon Phillips, who has dedicated years to
caring for injured and orphaned animals, and
for Edel Wignell, who loves platypuses almost
as much as bilbies
M. J.

First U.S. edition 2016

Library of Congress Catalog Card Number 2015932372
ISBN 978-0-7636-8098-5

15 16 17 18 19 20 TWP 10 9 8 7 6 5 4 3 2 1

Printed in Johor Bahru, Malaysia

This book was typeset in Journal and Myriad Pro.
The illustrations were created with mixed media.

Candlewick Press
99 Dover Street
Somerville, Massachusetts 02144

visit us at www.candlewick.com

Thank you to the Australian Reptile Park, Somersby,
for their wonderful help with my research.
S. W.

PLATYPUS

SUE WHITING   illustrated by MARK JACKSON

CANDLEWICK PRESS

Beyond the snaking bend in the creek, where the water lazes in a still green pool, a scraggly gum tree perches on the edge of the bank. Its tangle of roots clings desperately to the earth, a catcher's mitt for fallen leaves and broken-off branches.

Cleverly hidden behind this mesh of debris is the entrance to a burrow, and poking out of this burrow is a wide duck-like bill. But the bill doesn't belong to a duck.

The creature in the burrow is one of the world's most puzzling animals. When British scientists first studied a specimen in 1799, it seemed so strange that they thought it was a fake.

Out of the burrow, a long furry animal emerges. He squeezes under the roots and lumbers awkwardly down the steep bank. The creature is low to the ground and has a wide tail like a beaver's. But it's not a beaver. What can it be?

This semiaquatic animal usually moves only short distances on land. It has squat legs that stick out from the side of its body. These legs are better adapted for digging and swimming than for walking.

This unusual creature is a platypus.

In the shade of the gum trees, the pool is calm and cool. Platypus plunges into the water. With only the top of his bill, head, and back gliding above the surface, he resembles a miniature crocodile.

Without warning, Platypus arches his back and disappears, diving deep, water streaming through his fur, tiny air bubbles following in his wake.

His webbed front feet fan out like paddles and stroke the water rhythmically: left, right, left, right.

Platypuses' bodies are sleek and on average are about sixteen to twenty inches (forty to fifty centimeters) long. They swim with their forelegs. Their hind legs and tail trail behind and help them to steer.

Platypus is foraging—the mud is his dinner table. Eyes and ears closed, he uses his bill to find his way and to locate food. Back and forth, back and forth, Platypus's bill swishes across the sludge.

Platypuses' bills are soft, rubbery, and very sensitive. They pick up the movement of other animals, a bit like radar.

Platypuses eat small water animals such as worms, insect larvae, crawfish, and beetles.

Hurrying.
Scurrying.
Always moving.
Always busy.
Always looking for a meal.
Platypus is perpetual motion—
never still.

He rises to the surface for air. But only the tiny nostril holes on the top of his bill nudge above the water. A quick breath, and he's back down again.

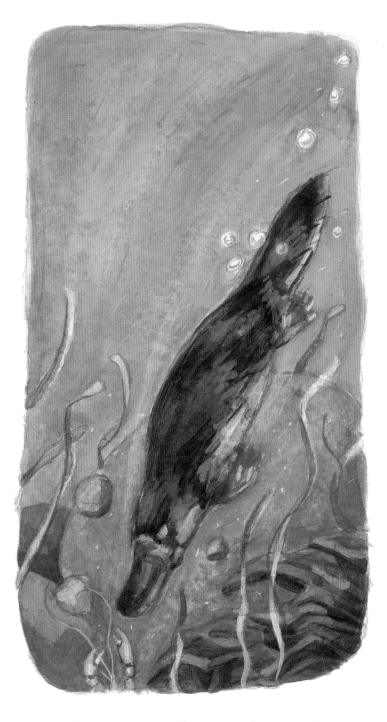

Platypuses usually stay submerged for about thirty seconds to a minute. They will dive repeatedly when foraging — sometimes more than seventy times in one hour!

Platypus senses a crawfish and gives chase. He pushes large river stones out of his way and bustles his bill under a rotting log. He is determined.

At last, he snares the crawfish and climbs onto a half-submerged rock to enjoy his snack.

Then he's off again.
It takes a lot to fill his belly.

Platypuses store their catches in pouches in
their cheeks till they come to the surface to eat.
Adult platypuses are toothless and grind their
food using stiff plates inside their bills.

Night settles in. Frogs croon to the starry sky. Thirsty wallabies appear at the creek edge to drink. Under the cover of darkness, Platypus rides the current, performs back flips, rolls over and over and over.

Hurrying. Scurrying. Always moving. Always busy. Always looking for a meal.

Platypuses forage for food about twelve hours
each day, mostly at night.

Their tails store most of their fat.
A thick firm tail is a sign of a
healthy platypus.

The stream flows over a bed of
smooth, round pebbles. Platypus
climbs onto a mossy log and has a
long scratch, his back claws working
hard at his velvety fur.

Platypuses spend a lot of time grooming their double-layered fur. The flat hair of the top layer is waterproof. The dense woolly underfur traps and holds air to keep the platypus warm.

There is movement on the shore, and Platypus feels threatened. It is too shallow to dive, so he slips off the log and hides beneath it. He could strike if cornered. But he lies low until it is safe for him to clamber over the rocks and into the next pool.

Male platypuses have venomous spurs behind their back legs. The venom is not deadly to humans, but it can cause severe pain.

Platypuses are one of the few venomous mammals in the world.

Up ahead, on the banks of this new pool, a female platypus is carrying leaves into her burrow. Deep inside are her nestlings, and she is intent on protecting them.

Our platypus glides on by. He isn't interested in the female. Mating season is over, and he has no need for company.

A female builds a separate nesting burrow. When her eggs are laid, she curls up in a nest in her burrow with her eggs pressed between her tail and stomach.

Darkness fades, and soon shafts of morning sun begin to slide through the water. Platypus swims back past the bend in the creek, back to his calm green pool. Back to his burrow behind the tangled roots of the straggly gum tree.

Platypuses spend most daylight hours in their burrows. The burrows are usually constructed into the earth on the side of the riverbank.

Once inside, he snuggles into the
warm earth and welcomes sleep.

Platypus is still at last.

THE PUZZLING PLATYPUS

The platypus is a puzzling animal. It has webbed feet and a bill like a duck, and fur and a tail like a beaver; is low to the ground and walks like a reptile; lays eggs like a bird; produces milk for its young like a mammal; and is venomous like a snake. How bizarre is that? It is classified as a monotreme—an egg-laying mammal. Platypuses and echidnas are the only monotremes on the planet.

Platypuses are found in freshwater rivers and streams in Tasmania and the eastern states of mainland Australia. They are secretive animals and seldom seen in the wild. Predators include snakes, foxes, and dingoes. However, their biggest threat is loss of habitat through drought, flooding, land clearing, and water pollution.

A female platypus lays one to three eggs.

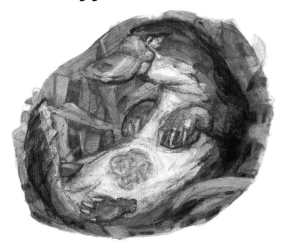

Once the babies hatch, they suckle milk from patches on her belly.

These nestlings stay in the burrow, suckling, for about three to four months before heading out to the river.

INDEX

Look up the pages to find out about all these platypus things.

Don't forget to look at both kinds of words — **this kind** and this kind.